A GUIDE TO YOM KIPPUR

By the same author

JEWISH PRAYER

WE HAVE REASON TO BELIEVE

A GUIDE TO
YOM KIPPUR

by

RABBI LOUIS JACOBS, B.A., Ph.D.

Minister, New West End Synagogue
London

JEWISH CHRONICLE PUBLICATIONS
London

Published by
JEWISH CHRONICLE PUBLICATIONS
37 *Furnival Street, London, EC4*

Made and printed in Great Britain by
THE SHARON PRESS
31 *Furnival Street, London, EC4*

CONTENTS

For my children

ISSUR YITZCHAK

NAOMI

DAVID ELIYAHU

CHAPTER I

YOM KIPPUR

Introduction

ON THIS awesome and joyful day of repentance, Jews gather in their Synagogues, their lives intermingled with the past of their people, re-living the tragedies of antiquity, re-enacting the ancient glories. During the long day the saints and martyrs, the poets and prophets of Israel come to life to sing again their song of triumph. Israel's sweet serenade to its God is heard above the strident noise of worldly pomp. Israel's spirit is vindicated before the world. The High Priest clad in white walks again in the Temple courts to offer atonement for his people; Akiba repeats his defiance of the mighty Roman Emperor by teaching the Torah to his faithful disciples; the power of the Crusaders is again set at naught as their victims recite the *Shema* with heads unbowed. On this day Israel draws inspiration from the past, looks towards its future and to the day of which the prophets dreamed when all men will worship the true God and his Kingdom will be established upon earth.

Other peoples have erected towering palaces, have built great bridges to span mighty rivers and wide roads to cross inhospitable deserts; they have produced fine art and moving music to stir the souls of men: the Jews created a day. A day of haunting beauty and spiritual power during which man is elevated far above his mundane concerns into the higher realms of the ideal. A day of peace and harmony and reconciliation, of prayer and reverence and awe when man comes face to face with God. A whimsical but profound Rabbinic calculation points out that the numerical value of the Hebrew letters of the word for Satan total three hundred and sixty four, one less than the number of days in the year. For on one day in the year the Satan of strife and contention, of coarseness and materialism, holds no sway over human affairs. On this day Israel is compared to the ministering angels in their sublime worship of the Lord of Hosts.

There can hardly be a Jew with soul so dulled that this day has lost its appeal for him. The Talmud speaks of a heavenly voice heard by sinners on *Yom Kippur* calling across the gulf dividing God from man: 'Return, ye back-sliding children.' Many Jews, estranged from the faith of their fathers, have heard that voice speaking to them in soothing, persuasive tones, encouraging them to believe that no one is excluded from before God's Presence and that His merciful hand is ever outstretched to receive His erring children who sincerely return to Him.

The significance of the day lies in its all-embracing character. No man is so good, so pious, so worthy as to be absolved from throwing himself on God's abundant mercies. No man is so depraved as to be incapable of invoking God's mercies. No man is so unlearned that his voice cannot be heard by God even if his knowledge of

Hebrew be so slender that the prayers have no meaning for him. There is a lovely Hasidic tale of a poor, untutored lad who brought with him to the Synagogue on *Yom Kippur* the whistle he used while watching his father's sheep. Unable to follow the prayers, the boy played his whistle in recognition of the glory of God. And all the great Rabbis present said that where their prayers had failed the simple, sincere tune of the shepherd boy had succeeded in opening the gates of Heaven.

Why One Day in the Year?

Sensitive people have a horror of parading their religious emotions, of wearing their heart on their sleeve. It sometimes appears to such people an affectation to set aside one day in the year for self-improvement and self-examination in the company of others. It seems to them to be adopting a pose, a pretence without feeling. Is it not hypocritical to devote one day in the year to prayer and introspection and forget all about these things during the rest of the year?

Put in this way, the question can have only one answer. *Yom Kippur* is chiefly of value for the effect it has on the lives of those who observe it, during the whole of the year. The idea of man mending his ways by approaching God with contrition in his heart must not be confined to a special day of judgment. A man is judged every day, every hour, every moment, said one of the Rabbis. Another saying in the same vein runs: 'He who says: "I will sin and *Yom Kippur* will atone for my sin" does not find atonement on *Yom Kippur*.'

But this is not to say that there is little value in the observance of a special day of repentance and communion with God. All peoples, at every stage of civilisation, have seen purpose in setting aside special days of commemoration. The accumulated wisdom of mankind testifies to the strength of an idea to which expression is given and homage paid by many people at the same time. There is nothing artificial in exposing ourselves to inspiration of one kind or another. If honesty only permitted us to laugh and cry at our own experiences we would never go to the theatre or the cinema. The late Rabbi Amiel, first Chief Rabbi of Tel Aviv, speaks, in one of his sermons, of *Yom Kippur* as a 'Temple in Time.' The metaphor is apt. God can be as little contained in a day as He can in a place. That *Yom Kippur* is relative to man's experience, not to God's, is expressed in the profound Midrashic saying that God asks the angels the date of judgment day and they reply: 'Let us go down and see when Israel observes it'! But just as men have found value in setting aside a house of worship for the God Who is outside space and Who embraces all space there is nothing incongruous about setting aside a portion of time for the concentrated worship of the God Who is outside time and Who embraces all time. For we humans inhabit space and time and we are influenced both by our surroundings and by periodic reminders of the truths we profess. In the view of the Rabbis, the Temple was erected that God should dwell in the hearts of the people moved by its impressive ritual. So, too, with *Yom Kippur*. God does not, as it were, come down to earth for only one day in the year. But the day, if observed in proper fashion, will have the effect of bringing man nearer to God in the year ahead.

In Bible Times

In the Bible, the central feature of the great day of atonement is the Temple ritual. On this day, we are told, the High Priest was to discard his garments of splendour and, wearing only the plain linen tunic, breeches, girdle and mitre of the common priest, he was to enter the Holy of Holies, the most sacred spot in the Sanctuary, there to atone for his own sins, those of his household and those of the whole community of Israel. Two goats were to be taken, upon which lots were to be cast, one for the Lord and one for Azazel. The goat chosen for the Lord was to be offered as a sacrifice. The other, the 'scapegoat,' was to be taken away to Azazel in the wilderness.

On this day the people were to 'afflict their souls' and refrain from all manner of work. It was to be a 'sabbath of solemn rest' and a 'statute for ever.' 'For on this day shall atonement be made for you, to cleanse you; from all your sins shall ye be clean before the Lord.' (*Lev.* xvi: 30)

The rite of the scapegoat has long puzzled Bible scholars and commentators. What was the purpose of sending the goat laden with the sins of the people to the wilderness? What was Azazel? How do we account for this rite, so unlike the usual practices, in the Temple service? These questions still await a conclusive reply and it seems as if, at this late date, we shall never know the full answer. It is possible, even exceedingly plausible, that the Torah, as in so many other cases, assimilated an ancient pagan practice to convey ideas of its own. The goat is not offered as a sacrifice to Azazel. The famous mediaeval commentator, Nahmanides, may have been very near to the truth when he interpreted the rite to mean that the goat was sent to the 'spirit of desolation' in order to symbolise for the Israelites the need for a complete break with sin, which brings utter ruin in its wake. Nahmanides is of the opinion that Azazel was the name of a goat-like demon (believed to inhabit the wilderness) to which people were wont to offer sacrifice. In order to purge the minds of its adherents of the base notion that Azazel had any objective reality the Torah uses this very name as the symbol of utter desolation and nothingness. Rabbinic teaching, on the other hand, takes Azazel to be the name of a strong mountain from which the goat was pushed to hurtle to its destruction. A later idea read into the account is that of 'giving the devil his due.' The goat is a sort of bribe to Satan. As a latter-day teacher said, the lesson we should derive from the account of the scapegoat is to give at least as much to God as we give to the devil!

But these and other theories do not solve the difficulty and the mystery remains. Certain it is that the worship of the wilderness demons is prohibited in the very next chapter of the book of Leviticus. Certain, too, that when in the subsequent history of Judaism evil was personified as Satan, that being was completely subordinate to God.

In the Rabbinic Literature

For the Rabbis, *Yom Kippur* was the great and holy day when Israel meets its God. *Yom Kippur* is judgment day, the culmination of the Ten Days of Penitence which begin with *Rosh Ha-Shanah*. The passage in Isaiah 'Seek ye the Lord while He may be found, Call ye upon Him while He is near' is applied by the Rabbis to the ten days beginning with *Rosh Ha-Shanah* and ending on *Yom Kippur* when God is very near. It was on *Yom Kippur*, say the Rabbis, that Moses came down from the mount with the second tablets of stone, bringing his people the good tidings that God had shewn mercy to them and had pardoned them for the sin of worshipping the golden calf.

The *Mishnah*, the great Code of Jewish Law compiled by Rabbi Judah the Prince at the end of the second century, records the accepted teaching that *Yom Kippur* atones only for sins committed against God, for religious sins. But for offences against his neighbour a man does not find atonement on *Yom Kippur* until he has pacified those he has offended.

Though the day is one of fasting and self-denial it is, for the Rabbis, a day of joy on which sin is pardoned and man reconciled with God. Rabban Simeon b. Gamaliel said that *Yom Kippur* was one of the two happiest days in the year for Israel when the daughters of Israel would go out in borrowed finery (borrowed, in order not to shame the girl who had no fine clothes of her own) and present themselves before the young men of their choice that they may propose to them. Some critics have displayed a complete lack of imagination and historical insight in suggesting that this saying be amended to read *Yom Ha-Purim* (the Day of Purim) instead of *Yom Ha-Kippurim*. The Rabbis had a more robust sense of what was fitting. There was nothing incongruous to them in young men using the holy day to make a proposal of marriage. For the Rabbis the setting up of a Jewish home was in the forefront of religious activities. Marriage was the first religious duty mentioned in the Torah. For them, too, there was no precise division between the secular and the sacred. The whole Rabbinic system was an attempt to sanctify the secular so that a proposal of marriage carried out in the right spirit could be a most praiseworthy action for the holiest day in the year. It was not until the destruction of the Temple and the bitter persecutions to which the Jews in the Middle Ages were subjected that the note of tragedy was heard in the liturgy of *Yom Kippur* and the more sombre mood came to prevail.

In Mediaeval and Modern Times

During the Middle Ages some of the finest religious hymns—*Piyyutim*—were composed for recitation on *Yom Kippur*. Many of these have become part of the standard liturgy of the day. By this period *Yom Kippur* had evolved as a day to be spent almost entirely in prayer and worship. Many Jews would not even return home on the night of *Kippur* but would prefer to spend it in the Synagogue chanting hymns and singing psalms until daybreak. Although in the ordinary way it was forbidden to sleep in the Synagogue, an exception was made on this day so as to enable those who spent the whole twenty four hours in the house of God to snatch some sleep. Most of the Rabbis, however, advised against the practice of a long night vigil if as a result the worshipper was drowsy during the prayers of the day. There is shrewd awareness of the need for a sense of proportion in this matter in the anecdote told of a niggardly rich man whose custom it was to spend the whole night of *Kippur* reciting Psalms in the Synagogue. Joseph Baer Soloweitchick of Brest-Litovsk (the much admired Lithuanian Rabbi of the last century) is said to have gone up to the man and accused him of being a deserter. 'A deserter, Rabbi, what do you mean?' 'In an army,' replied the Rabbi, 'there are many different kinds of soldiers, each with his own task to perform. If an infantryman goes over without permission to the cavalry he is a deserter from his post and can endanger the lives of his comrades just as much as the man who deserts from the whole field of battle. Reciting Psalms on *Yom Kippur* when the congregation has gone home to sleep is a suitable occupation for the poor man who can serve God in few other ways. Your duty is to go home and sleep well but to resolve to be more generous with your wealth in the future. Otherwise your recital of Psalms is nothing more than a cloak for your miserliness.'

In the famous Lithuanian Yeshiboth of the last and of

this century the whole month preceding *Yom Kippur* was a period of intense concentration on Torah study and self-improvement. Former students would leave their homes and return to their *alma mater* for the season. Here they would listen to moralistic talks on the duties of man and his relationship with God and here they would try to recapture some of the enthusiasm of their youth for the Torah and its teachings. At these sessions they would learn to know something of what is meant by *Yirath Shamayim*—the Fear of Heaven—a concept so lacking in much of modern Judaism that we are almost ashamed to speak of it. Perhaps this is because of the pietistic and somewhat sanctimonious overtones the concept has acquired but we can only dispense with the idea itself at the cost of impoverishing our religious life.

The *Hasidim*, in particular, attached much importance to the ten days beginning with *Rosh Ha-Shanah*. From far and wide the followers of the 'Rebbe' would flock to his 'court', there to take part in the *Rosh Ha-Shanah* and *Yom Kippur* services, the most important of which were generally conducted by the Rebbe himself. Numerous are the tales told of how the Hasidic leaders would behave on the holy day. The accounts of how Levi Yitzchak of Berditchev (*d.* 1809), the renowned Hasidic leader, pleaded for his people on *Yom Kippur* before the Throne of God, have become part of the folk-lore of the Jewish people. In the stories of this lovable character arguing with God there re-occurs the *motif*, found in the Bible in the account of Abraham's plea for the sinners of Sodom and Moses' intercession for his people, of the just man confronting God with His own truth, as a favoured child pleads with his father. It is said that Levi Yitzchak once asked a tailor after *Yom Kippur*: 'Since you could not read the prayers on *Yom Kippur*, what did you do?' The tailor replied: 'I said to God: "Dear God, I confess that I have sinned. I confess that there have been times when I failed to return to the customers the left-over cloth. When I could not help it I even ate food that was not strictly *kosher*. But take Yourself, God! Just examine Your sins. You have taken children away from their mothers and mothers from their children. You have reduced so many to poverty and want. So, You see, that Your sins are more serious than mine. I'll tell You what, God! Let's strike a bargain! You forgive me and I'll forgive You".' When Levi Yitzchak heard this he said that the tailor had let off God too lightly. For this simple man in his innocent faith had been in a position to compel God to redeem His people!

A specially fascinating chapter in the annals of Jewish religious experience concerns the large number of men in modern times who have been converted to a new view of life and whose whole mental outlook has been transformed as a result of what Rudolph Otto calls the 'numinous' quality of *Yom Kippur*. Otto coined the word (from the Latin *numen*, divine will) to describe the feelings of awe characteristic of man's communion with God. *Rosh Ha-Shanah* and *Yom Kippur* are called in Jewish traditional teaching *Yomim Noraim*, which is better translated as 'Days of Awe' than 'Days of Fear.' They are days when the sense of the numinous is specially strong. C. S. Lewis has well explained the concept of the *numinous* as follows. If you become aware that there is a lion in the room with you, you are afraid. Your fear is caused by your knowledge of the possibility that the lion may harm you. If, on the other hand, you are aware that a ghost is in the room, your fear is of a different order. Here the terror is caused by the presence of the uncanny and unknown itself, not by the harm it may do. Similarly, the 'fear of God' is not fear of what God may do to the sinner but the tremendous feeling of unworthiness and insignificance that man feels when confronted with the Presence of the Lord of the Universe. Otto, in his famous book *The Idea of the Holy*, refers to the liturgy of *Rosh Ha-Shanah* and *Yom Kippur* as rich in the concept of the *numinous*. It is well known that Otto, in fact, conceived his notion of the tremendous and awe-inspiring as an important factor in religion because of his participation in a *Yom Kippur* service in a simple North African Synagogue.

Perhaps the two best known examples of religious conversion after *Yom Kippur* worship are those of Aimé Pallière and Franz Rosenzweig. Aimé Pallière (1875-1954), author of *The Unknown Sanctuary*, was born into a devout French Catholic family. He became a convert to Judaism in theory, if not in practice (his Rabbi advised him against fully embracing the Jewish faith, believing that he could best further the Jewish ideal from without) through pondering the teachings of Judaism and through visits to the Synagogue, particularly on *Yom Kippur* when Jewish spirituality was to be seen in its most intense mood. Franz Rosenzweig (1886-1929) was the son of an assimilated German Jewish family and in his youth had resolved to embrace Christianity. But being a man of the staunchest intellectual honesty he wanted first to know more about the faith he intended leaving. He attended Synagogue services on *Yom Kippur* in preparation for the Church! 'Rosenzweig,' says his biographer and friend, Nahum Glatzer, 'left the Synagogue a changed person. What he had thought he could find in the Church only—faith that gives one an orientation in the world—he found on that day in the Synagogue.'

A Jew must indeed be spiritually insensitive to remain unmoved at the thought that in the Synagogue on *Yom Kippur* he is at one with his co-religionists everywhere who stand as he does before the judgment seat of God. That he is united with the Jew in every corner of the world, with the pious Jew who attends services three times a day and with the Jew who never enters the Synagogue at any other time in the year, with the scholar who knows half the Talmud by heart and with the unlearned who cannot even recite the Shema in Hebrew, all of them with a common purpose and common aim. 'Thou art One and Thy name is One and Who is like unto Thy people Israel a unique nation upon earth.'

The Name

The name *Yom Kippur* is the Rabbinic version of the Biblical (plural form) *Yom Ha-Kippurim*. *Yom* means day and the root meaning of *Kippur*, *Kippurim* and *Kapparah* (the form most frequently used for 'atonement') is 'to scour,' 'to cleanse thoroughly,' 'to erase.' Sin is thought of as a stain to be removed if the soul is to appear pure before its Creator. Another possible meaning of the root is 'to cover.' In atonement sin is covered, is hidden out of sight. *Yom Kippur* is then the day of cleansing from sin, the day on which Israel once again finds favour in the eyes of God. Repentance is an essential preliminary to *Kapparah*. Only one of the Talmudic Rabbis (Judah the Prince) taught that the day itself is endowed with the power of erasing sin and his view is not accepted. To ask for God's forgiveness without repenting of the wrong he has done is as if (to use the favourite Rabbinic metaphor) a man, in Temple times, immerses himself in the purifying waters of the spring while holding fast to the reptile which contaminates. Repentance can be compared to the child's burning need to say he is sorry when he has done wrong. *Kapparah* is the parent's embrace to shew that all is forgiven. Repentance is man's approach to God; *Kapparah* is God's response.

CHAPTER 2

FASTING

Fasting

'In the seventh month, on the tenth day of the month, ye shall afflict your souls.' (*Lev.* xvi.: 29) From this verse the duty of fasting on *Yom Kippur* is derived. From the earliest times 'afflicting the soul' was understood to mean fasting. It is of interest in this connection that when the prophet speaks of 'afflicting the soul' (in the portion read as the *Haphtorah* on *Yom Kippur* morning) he does so as a synonym for fasting.

> '*Wherefore have we fasted, and Thou seest not?*
> *Wherefore have we afflicted our soul, and Thou takest no knowledge?*'
> *Behold, in the day of your fast ye pursue your business,*
> *And exact all your labours.* (Isaiah, lviii: 3)

In a number of Biblical passages fasting is mentioned in association with prayer and repentance. When the prophet Elijah rebukes King Ahab for his sin, the book of Kings records that 'when Ahab heard those words, that he rent his clothes, and put sackcloth upon his flesh, and fasted, and lay in sackcloth, and went softly.'

When David's child was dying he spent his days and nights in prayer and fasting. And in the book of Joel when the people are urged to repent, the admonition is conveyed in these words: 'Yet even now, saith the Lord, Turn ye unto Me with all your heart, And with fasting, and with weeping, and with lamentation.'

When Jonah is sent by God to preach repentance to the great city of Nineveh the book of Jonah tells us: 'And the people of Nineveh believed God; and they proclaimed a fast, and put on sackcloth, from the greatest of them even to the least of them. And the tidings reached the King of Nineveh, and he arose from his throne, and laid his robe from him, and covered him with sackcloth, and sat in ashes. And he caused it to be proclaimed and published through Nineveh by the decree of the king and nobles, saying: "Let neither man nor beast, herd nor flock, taste any thing; let them not feed, nor drink water; but let them be covered with sackcloth, both man and beast, and let them cry mightily unto God; yea, let them turn every one from his evil way, and from the violence that is in their hands. Who knoweth whether God will not turn and repent, and turn away from His fierce anger, that we perish not." And God saw their works, that they turned from their evil way; and God repented of the evil, which He said He would do unto them; and He did it not.'

When the returned exiles renewed their covenant with God under the leadership of Ezra it is said that they 'were assembled with fasting and with sackcloth, and earth upon them' and before Esther entered the king's presence to plead for the life of her people she sent messengers to Mordecai to say to him: 'Go, gather together all the Jews that are present in Shushan, and fast ye for me, and neither eat nor drink three days, night or day; I also and my maidens will fast in like manner; and so will I go in unto the king, which is not according to the law; and if I perish, I perish.'

The Rabbis list certain other 'afflictions' to be practised on *Yom Kippur* in addition to fasting. In the words of the Mishnah: 'On the Day of Atonement, eating, drinking, washing, anointing, putting on sandals, and marital intercourse are forbidden.'

Another reason given for not wearing shoes of leather on *Yom Kippur* is that these can only be fashioned after an animal has been killed and as God's mercy is over all His creatures it is not fitting to wear leather on the day when we pray for mercy.

Why Fast?

Four main reasons are given for the command to fast on *Yom Kippur*:

(a) *Fasting as a penance*

The most obvious reason for fasting on *Yom Kippur* is that by this means we shew contrition for the wrong we have done and the good we have failed to do. The man who 'punishes himself' may be morbidly masochistic. But most people feel the need to give of themselves, to make some sacrifice, in order to demonstrate that their protestations of remorse mean something and are more than lip service. Self-affliction (Judaism does not encourage the excess of this) in moderation is an act affirming a man's sincerity. The man who fasts for his sins is saying in so many words, I do not want to be let off lightly; I deserve to be punished.

(b) *Fasting as self-discipline*

Self-indulgence and lack of self-control frequently lead to sin. It is natural that repentance be preceded by an attempt at self-discipline. Disciplining oneself is never easy but all religious teachers have insisted on its value. It is true that history and literature abound in examples of the harm done by an over-active Puritan conscience, especially when it seeks to interfere with the behaviour of others. Macaulay said that the Puritans objected to bear-baiting not because it gave pain to the bear but because it gave pleasure to the spectators! But the value of self-discipline must not be judged by its aberrations. The traditional Jewish character ideal is for a person to be harsh with himself but indulgent towards others. Fasting on *Yom Kippur* serves as a potent reminder for the need of the self-discipline which leads to self-improvement.

(c) *Fasting as a means of focussing the mind on the spiritual*

It has been noted frequently that Judaism frankly recognises the bodily instincts and the need for their legitimate gratification. This is best illustrated in the Rabbinic comment on the verse in the book of Genesis that God saw all that He had created and behold it was very good—not simply *good*, remark the Rabbis, but *very good*. Good refers to the good inclination; very good, to the evil inclination. For, the Rabbis go on to say, were it not for the bodily instincts life would be good but it would be a colourless, unvarying good. A man would have no ambitions, he would not build a house or marry, the world would be left desolate. And yet with all its recognition of the bodily needs, religion seeks to encourage and foster the spiritual side of man's life. By fasting on *Yom Kippur* the needs of the body are left unattended for twenty four hours and the Jew gives all his concentration to the things of the spirit. This is the meaning of the references in Jewish tradition that Jews are compared to the angels on *Yom Kippur* when, clothed in white, they spend the whole day in prayer, contemplation and worship.

We must, of course, live in this world. 'One world at a time' is sound Jewish doctrine. But unless our faith is to be denuded of its spirituality we must, from time to time, direct our thoughts to the non-physical side of existence. Scripture says that 'no man shall be in the tent of meeting' (*Lev*. xvi: 17) when the High Priest enters to make atonement there on *Yom Kippur*. This is taken by the *Midrash* to mean that at that awful hour the High Priest was 'no man', his body became ethereal like that of the angels. This is what happens to every Jew who observes the day as it should be observed.

(d) *Fasting as a means of awakening compassion*

By knowing what it means to go hungry, albeit for a day, our hearts are moved for those who suffer. By fasting we are moved to think of the needs of others and to alleviate their suffering. In the *Yom Kippur* morning *Haphtorah* this idea is given its classic expression. The prophet Isaiah castigates his people for their neglect of the poor. Their fasting and their pretence of piety is not acceptable to God if it serves merely as a cloak for inhumanity:

Is not this the fast that I have chosen?
To loose the fetters of wickedness,
To undo the bands of the yoke,
And to let the oppressed go free,
And that ye break every yoke?
Is it not to deal thy bread to the hungry,
And that thou bring the poor that are cast out to thy house?
When thou seest the naked, that thou cover him,
And that thou hide not thyself from thine own flesh?

CHAPTER 3

LAWS AND CUSTOMS OF YOM KIPPUR

The White Fast

It is unfortunate that our non-Jewish friends sometimes speak of *Yom Kippur* as the 'Black Fast.' *Yom Kippur* in Jewish tradition is a day of solemnity but it is also a day of joy, a festive day. A more appropriate name would be the 'White Fast.' The ark in the Synagogue is draped in white. So, too, are the Scrolls of the Law and the reading desk. Many people wear the white robe known as the *kittel* (originally white was worn because Israel on *Kippur* resemble the angelic hosts who are 'clothed in white'; only at a later date was the white robe worn on this day identified with the shrouds worn by the dead, as a reminder of man's mortality). White is the colour of purity. 'Come now, and let us reason together, Saith the Lord; Though your sins be as scarlet, They shall be as white as snow; Though they be red like crimson, They shall be as wool.' (*Isaiah* i: 18)

Great writers have dwelled on the emotions aroused by the colour white. It is the colour of refinement and beauty and the ghastly hue striking terror in the hearts of those who behold it. White both attracts and repels. It is the most effective colour to symbolise the unfathomable and the mysterious. To use Otto's phrase it is a 'numinous' colour, eminently suitable for the day of *Kippur*. White, as Chesterton has finely said in a famous essay, is not a mere absence of colour; it is a shining and affirmative thing, as fierce as red, as definite as black. Virtue, symbolised by white, is not the mere absence of vices or the avoidance of moral dangers, it is a vivid and separate thing. In the *Kabbalah* white is the colour of peace, mercy and pity.

Kapparoth

The Babylonian (post-Talmudic) scholars refer to (and generally condemn as superstitious) the curious practice of taking a cockerel on the eve of *Yom Kippur*, waving it three times round the head while reciting Scriptural verses, and then slaughtering and eating it or giving it to the poor to eat. The purpose behind the rite is to provide a symbolic sacrifice, following that interpretation of the ancient sacrificial system which sees it as a representation of what ought to have happened to the sinner were it not for God's mercy. Although the rite found many able defenders, teachers like Solomon Ibn Adret (1235-1310) sought to discourage it as pagan and superstitious. The author of the *Shulchan Aruch*, the standard Code of Jewish law and practice, follows Adret but most of the later writers accept the custom. Many present-day teachers suggest that the custom be followed but that it should be performed with money which is waved round the head while reciting the formula: 'This money will be given to charity and I will enter a year of life and peace.' The money is then distributed to the poor. In some Synagogues special charity plates, inscribed with the names of worthy causes, are laid out on the eve of *Yom Kippur* into which the Kapparoth money is placed.

Reconciliation

It is customary on the eve of *Kippur* to ask one's friends and acquaintances for forgiveness for any wrongs done to them during the past year. The day of reconciliation with God must be preceded by reconciliation among men.

The Festive Meal

It is a *mitzvah*, a religious duty, to eat well on the eve of *Yom Kippur*. Only easily digested food should be partaken of at the final meal before the fast. At this meal the piece of bread over which grace before meals is recited should be dipped in honey while the prayer is recited: 'May God grant that the year ahead be a good and sweet one.' The obvious reason for eating well is to gain strength for the fast, to prepare for the rigours of the coming day. But another reason has been given. *Yom Kippur* is a *Yom Tob*, a festival, a day of joy, because on it Israel is reconciled with God. On all the other festivals of the year the Jew is commanded to make merry, to eat and drink in honour of the occasion. As this is impossible on *Yom Kippur*, the festive meal is partaken of on the preceding day. It demonstrates the fundamental sanity and life-affirming attitude of Judaism. The one fast day in the year enjoined by the Torah is preceded (and followed, according to custom) by a feast.

Blessing of the Children

Before proceeding to the Synagogue, the father of the house blesses his children with the traditional blessing: 'God make thee as Ephraim and Manasseh' to boys; 'God make thee as Sarah, Rebekah, Rachel and Leah' to girls. 'The Lord bless thee and keep thee; the Lord make his face to shine upon thee, and be gracious unto thee; the Lord turn his face unto thee and give thee peace.'

Honouring the Day

Sabbath garments should be worn on *Yom Kippur* in honour of the day. For the same reason the table in the home should be covered with a white cloth as on the Sabbath and the festival candles should be kindled.

Prohibition of Work

Yom Kippur is described in the Bible as the Sabbath of Sabbaths. Consequently it is forbidden to do all manner of work on this day.

Handling of Food

If possible food should not even be handled on *Yom Kippur* though, of course, an exception is made for those who have to give their children to eat.

Should Children Fast?

Children under the age of nine should not be allowed to fast even for a few hours. But from this age they should be trained to fast by postponing their breakfast for an hour or two longer each year.

A Sick Person on Yom Kippur

The rules of fasting on *Yom Kippur* are set aside where there is danger to life. Consequently when the doctor orders a person to eat on *Yom Kippur*, if he is not to jeopardise his chances of recovery, he must do so. Even if the doctor says that the sick person may fast without coming to harm but the person feels strongly that to fast may endanger his life, he may eat. The proper procedure for a person obliged to eat on *Yom Kippur* should be to consult a Rabbi who will advise him. It is said that Rabbi Hayyim Soloweitchick (*d.* 1918) was more lenient than other Rabbis with regard to sick people eating on *Yom Kippur*. He was fond of saying: 'It is not that I am lenient with regard to *Yom Kippur*, but I am strict with regard to saving life.' Grace before and after meals should be recited when a sick person eats on *Yom Kippur*. He should refer to *Yom Kippur* in the *Yaaleh veyabo* addition to the grace after meals.

The Night After Yom Kippur

The night following *Yom Kippur* is a minor festival. The *Midrash* says that after the long day of fasting has come to a close a heavenly voice proclaims: 'Go thy way, eat thy bread with joy, And drink thy wine with a merry heart; For God hath already accepted thy works.' (*Eccl.* ix: 7)

CHAPTER 4

THE HISTORY AND STRUCTURE OF THE SERVICES THE EVENING PRAYERS

The History and Structure of the Services

The Order of Service for *Yom Kippur* contains prayers which were recited in Temple times together with those composed by liturgical poets in the late middle ages. The Festival Prayer Book must not be thought of as the composition of one man or the product of one age. The earliest prayers are separated from the latest by a period of almost two thousand years.

The actual origin of the liturgy is veiled in obscurity. The Institution of the Synagogue is generally dated from the Babylonian Exile (586–539 BCE) but we have little information on the order of service in the ancient Synagogue. The earliest parts of the service appear to have been the readings from the Scroll of the Torah and the recitation of the Shema. Around these the services, as we know them, developed. By the period of the Mishnah (compiled about 200 CE) every daily congregational service consisted of the Amidah ('the standing prayer') with the addition of the Shema and its special benedictions in the morning and evening. The three daily prayers—morning, afternoon and evening—were said to correspond to three distinct parts of the Temple ritual (the morning offering, the afternoon offering and the burning of the offering on the altar in the evening) or to the three Patriarchs, Abraham, Isaac and Jacob. Various psalms and hymns were added from time to time until the prayer book emerged in its present form. Special prayers referring to the occasion were added on the festivals.

Including the service on the night of *Kippur*, there are five services of the day. The following is a bird's-eye view of the structure of these services.

1 EVENING SERVICE

The Evening Service begins with the formula granting permission 'to pray with the sinners' (see further) and with *Kol Nidre*. The ordinary evening service follows with the *Shema* and its benedictions and the *Yom Kippur Amidah*, to which is appended the confession of sin. Various hymns of later origin are then recited and the confession repeated. The service concludes with the *Abinu Malkenu* prayer.

2 MORNING SERVICE

(*a*) This follows the pattern of the Sabbath morning service, namely the daily benedictions, psalms, the *Shema* and *Amidah* and the Reader's repetition of the *Amidah* with the addition of special *Yom Kippur* hymns and songs of praise. The Ark is opened and two Scrolls taken from it for the *Yom Kippur* readings. The *Haphtorah* (the prophetic portion) is recited by a member of the congregation.

(*b*) After the prayer for the Royal Family and for the State of Israel the Memorial Service for the departed is recited. The Scrolls are then returned to the Ark.

3 THE ADDITIONAL SERVICE

On Sabbaths and Festivals an additional service is recited, describing the offerings brought in the Temple on the day. Like every other *Amidah* of *Yom Kippur* the Additional *Amidah* on *Kippur* concludes with the confession of sin. The Reader then repeats the *Amidah* during which *Yom Kippur* hymns are recited. A prominent feature in the repetition is the *Abhodah*—the account of the ancient Temple ritual. As a result of the fierce persecutions to which Jews in the Middle Ages were subjected a number of laments and dirges have been added to this part of the service emphasising the difference between former glories and present degradation. The confession is again recited and the service concludes with the Priestly Blessing and the prayer that Israel's supplications be acceptable before God.

4 AFTERNOON READINGS AND SERVICE

The Ark is opened once again and the Scroll taken from it. After the Torah reading a member of the congregation reads the book of Jonah as the *Haphtorah*.

The Scroll is returned to the Ark and the Afternoon *Amidah* is recited. The Reader then repeats the *Amidah*. Both in the *Amidah* and in the Reader's repetition the confession of sin is recited.

5 THE NEILAH PRAYER

On *Yom Kippur* a special *Amidah*—the *Neilah* prayer

(see further, Chapter 6) is added. The *Neilah Amidah* is recited and the Reader repeats the *Amidah*. The confession of sin in this *Amidah* differs in its wording from other confessions of the day. *Neilah* concludes with the Reader and Congregation reciting in a loud voice the *Shema* and the verses: 'Blessed be his glorious, sovereign Name for ever and ever,' and: 'The Lord he is God.'

THE EVENING PRAYER

Yom Kippur is now ended but the Congregation recites the week-day evening prayer before leaving the Synagogue. At the end of this prayer the *Shofar* is sounded.

Short notes will now be given in this and the following two chapters on some of the more important prayers and hymns of the day. The confessions of sin are dealt with separately in Chapter 7. (*Page references are to the Routledge and Shapiro Vallentine editions of the Festival Prayer Book.* No notes are given on those prayers such as the *Shema* which are recited on other days. Dr. Hertz's Commentary to the *Siddur* contains much useful information on these.)

בִּישִׁיבָה שֶׁל מַעְלָה

By Authority of the Court on High (R.15 and S.12)

The *Kol Nidre* service begins with the recital of this formula by the Reader and two elders of the congregation. The formula is traced to Rabbi Meir ben Baruch of Rothenburg (b. *c.*1220; *d.* 1293) and consists of permission granted to 'pray with them that have transgressed.' This is based on a Talmudic saying that a fast in which none of the sinners of Israel participate is no fast (i.e. the whole community of Israel, sinners as well as saints, must take part in Israel's reconciliation with God).

כָּל נִדְרֵי

Kol Nidre (R.15 and S.12)

A man's word is sacred. This is the idea behind the vow. A promise must be kept. In Biblical times a vow might be made to carry out a certain act or to abstain from carrying out a certain act, generally for the purpose of self-discipline, e.g. a vow to abstain from wine or strong drink. Some of the Rabbis favoured the attempt at reinforcement of one's resolutions for good by means of the vow but others looked upon it with disapproval. 'It is sufficient for thee that which the Torah forbids' is a typical Talmudic saying.

The Talmud rules that a declaration made at the beginning of the year cancelling all vows that will be made during the coming year has the effect of rendering those vows null and void. In due course (before the ninth century) a special formula, the *Kol Nidre* (*Kol*=all, *Nidre*=the vows), was introduced in Aramaic, the vernacular of the day. Despite much opposition on the part of many scholars the formula came to stay. The haunting melody which gives the *Kol Nidre* its tremendous appeal is of uncertain, but later, origin. The bitter years of Jewish persecution, the degradation of sin, the hope of repentance, the yearning of the estranged soul for reconciliation with God, all these find their expression in the melody. It has been noted that the tune possesses three *motifs*—first a note of pain and remorse, then a note of resolution and finally a note of triumph, corresponding to the three stages of repentance.

Jewish law does not know of the annulment of vows and promises made to others. The *Kol Nidre* has reference only to private vows, to promises affecting the self, e.g. a promise to abstain from food. Yet throughout the ages ignorant Jew-haters have claimed that the oath of the Jew was unreliable because he annuls all his vows with the *Kol Nidre* formula. Bigotry in this way justified the introduction of the infamous *more Judaico*, a special form of oath for the Jew in the Law Courts of the Middle Ages. A Byzantine law of the tenth century required a Jew while swearing to have a girdle of thorns round his loins and to stand in water. By a German code Jews had to stand on a sow's hide while taking the oath, and in the fifteenth century the law of Silesia required him to stand 'on a three-legged stool, pay a fine each time he falls, and lose his case if he falls four times.'

In view of these facts, Dr. J. H. Hertz was undoubtedly right when he argued that for Jews to give up the recitation of the *Kol Nidre* on the grounds of misunderstandings it gives rise to is for them tacitly to admit that the Jew-baiters were right that our ancestors' word was not to be trusted.

מַעֲרִיב

Maariv (R.18-30 and S.15-32)

The *Yom Kippur Maariv* includes the *Shema* and its benedictions, the *Amidah* and the special confession of sin (on this see Chapter 7). A special feature of this service (and of the morning service) is the recital of the second verse of the *Shema*: 'Blessed be his glorious, sovereign Name for ever and ever' in a loud voice. During the rest of the year this verse is recited silently.

Two reasons are given in the traditional sources for this custom. In the Pentateuch 'Blessed be . . . ' does not occur. But legend has it that when the patriarch, Jacob, called his sons to him before his death he said: 'My grandfather, Abraham, had an unworthy son. My father, Isaac, had an unworthy son. Perhaps one of my sons too is unworthy.' Whereupon all twelve sons proclaimed 'Hear, O Israel: the Lord our God, the Lord is One.' When Jacob heard this he exclaimed: 'Blessed be his glorious, sovereign Name for ever and ever.'

We, too, therefore repeat this verse in the *Shema*. But because Moses did not say it we repeat it silently out of respect for Moses, except on *Yom Kippur* when God's Name is especially honoured among the children of Israel. The other reason given is that this verse is the song of the angels. Humans dare not recite it aloud. But on *Yom Kippur* when Israel is compared to the angels it may be recited in a loud voice.

יַעֲלֶה

Yaaleh (R.31 and S.32-33)

This hymn of unknown origin begins each of its clauses with a letter of the alphabet, from *Tav*, the last letter, to *Aleph*, the first. It is obviously based on the three words of the special festival prayer *yaaleh, veyabo, veyeraeh*—'may it (our prayer) ascend, come to Thee and be seen by Thee.'

סְלַח נָא

Selah Na (R.36-37 and S.38-39)

Another alphabetical acrostic composed by Meir ben Baruch of Rothenburg (*c.*1220-1293), based on the opening two words *Selah Na* (Forgive, I beseech Thee) of Moses' prayer of intercession for his people. Meir of Rothenburg, one of the foremost Talmudists of his day, wrote numerous Responsa (about 1,500 of these have been preserved) on all branches of Jewish law in reply to queries addressed to him from many Jewish communities. Towards the end of his life he was held to ransom by order of the Emperor Rudolph and confined in the fortress of Ensisheim. The Rabbi refused to allow the Jewish Community to pay the ransom fearing that this would encourage extortion from Jews by holding men of learning to ransom. He died in the fortress where his body was kept for fourteen years until a wealthy Jew of Frankfort redeemed it asking only in return that his body should be buried next to the scholar. This wish was carried out.

אָמְנָם כֵּן

Omnam Ken (R.38 and S.41)

This poem uses rhyme in addition to the usual acrostic (Zangwill's translation in the *Festival Prayer Book* has skilfully captured the rhyming method). The author is unknown though Joseph Jacobs has tried to identify him with the martyr of York, R. Yom-Tob. When the Crusaders besieged York, Yom-Tob, the Rabbi of the city, exhorted his fellow-Jews to kill themselves rather than fall into the hands of their enemies and be compelled to forsake the faith of their fathers. The martyrdom at York took place on the eve of the Sabbath before Passover in the year 1190.

כִּי הִנֵּה כַּחֹמֶר

Ki Hine Kahomer (R.39 and S.42-43)

In this hymn of unknown authorship God is described as a craftsman shaping man's destiny. He is compared to the potter who moulds the plastic clay into various shapes; to the mason hewing the block of stone; to the smith bending the rigid steel; to the pilot casting his anchor into the sea; to the glass-blower, fashioning his vessels out of glass; to the embroiderer weaving intricate patterns in the robe; and to the silversmith removing the dross from the precious metal.

It is worthy of note that in all the illustrations given, the craftsman, no matter how skilled he may be, cannot produce a thing of beauty unless his raw material is good. It is sound Jewish teaching which thinks of God helping us to make our lives dignified and worthy. We have to provide Him, as it were, with the raw material. We have to give Him something to work on.

Seen in this light our abasement before God on *Yom Kippur* is to fall before Him that He may elevate us. It is the submission of the clay to the potter who can fashion it into a thing of beauty, of the silver to the refiner to purge it of its dross, of the ship to the pilot to guide it on its way.

אֵל מֶלֶךְ יוֹשֵׁב

The Thirteen Attributes (R.40 and frequently, also S.43-44)

During *Yom Kippur*, towards the end of each of the five services, the prayer beginning with 'Almighty King, who sittest upon a throne of mercy' is recited. This prayer refers to the Biblical account of how God appeared to Moses telling him that his people's sin was pardoned and recounting the thirteen attributes of divine mercy. The Bible does not speak of thirteen attributes but much is made of this classification in the Talmud. An idea found particularly in the writings of Maimonides and reflected in many Rabbinic teachings is that if man follows these attributes of mercy in his personal life, i.e. if he, like his Maker, is compassionate, merciful, gracious, truth loving and so on, God will shew mercy to him.

אָבִינוּ מַלְכֵּנוּ

Abinu Malkenu (R.55-57; Part II, pp. 104-106, 269-270; and S.62-65 and 236-239)

Each sentence in this prayer of supplication begins with the words *Abinu Malkenu* (Our Father! Our King!). God is described as the merciful father full of compassion for his children. But religious faith to be at all meaningful must present a constant challenge, calling out the best in its adherents. Hence God is described, too, as the king who makes demands on his subjects, and for whom his subjects have feelings of reverence and awe. The origin of the prayer is in the Talmudic account of how the great Akiba used the words in his request for rain: 'Our Father! Our King! We have no King besides Thee. Our Father! Our King! Have mercy upon us! Our Father! Our King! Act unto us for Thy name's sake!' Later on many additional verses were added but we cannot say with any degree of certainty when the prayer assumed its present form.

שִׁיר הַיִּחוּד

Hymn of Unity (R.60-72 and S.66-95)

This hymn originated in the circle of Judah the Saint (*d.* 1217), the author of the Book of the Devout, and is divided into seven parts, one for each day of the week. On festivals the appropriate portion is read on each day but as *Yom Kippur* cannot fall on a Sunday, a Tuesday or a Friday the portions for these days are omitted from the festival prayer book (though in some congregations the whole of the Hymn of Unity is recited after the service on *Yom Kippur* eve).

שִׁיר הַכָּבוֹד

Hymn of Glory (R.73-74 and S.96-97a)

This hymn, too, was composed in the circle of Judah the Saint. The hymn of glory is in the alphabet acrostic form and is in rhymed verse (Zangwill's translation captures the flavour of the original with great felicity). In many rites the hymn is recited each day, in others on the Sabbath only and some recite it only on *Rosh Ha-Shanah* and *Yom Kippur*. This latter was the view of the Gaon of Vilna (1720-1797) who considered the sentiments expressed in the hymn to be too exalted for frequent use.

CHAPTER 5

THE MORNING AND MUSAPH PRAYERS

Early Morning Service (R.1-53 and S.98-157)

The early morning service is the same as that of the Sabbath with the addition of the hymns on God's forgiveness (R.35; S.134) and on the verse 'Blessed be his glorious Name' (R.39; S.139). The *Amidah* is the *Yom Kippur Amidah* as recited at the evening service.

אֲמָּיךְ נָשָׂאתִי

The Reader's Supplication (R.53-54 and S.158-159)

The Reader's supplication at the beginning of the repetition of the *Amidah* was composed by the liturgical poet Meshullam ben Kalonymous, called 'The Great,' of Germany (end of 10th century). Meshullam was the author of polemical writings against the Karaites, the sect which denied the authority of the Talmud, basing its religious ideas and practices on the letter of the Bible. The idea behind the prayer is the unworthiness of man to stand before God as the messenger of the congregation. The Reader prays that God may give him strength to carry out his exalted task without faltering and win forgiveness for those who have appointed him to lead them in prayer.

אַתָּה הוּא אֱלֹהֵינוּ

Thou Art Our God (R.57-58 and S.164)

This hymn, too, is by Meshullam ben Kalonymous. Each half-line begins with a letter of the alphabet from *Aleph* to *Tav*. It was Heine who said that Jews pray in metaphysics. The hymn recounts the attributes of God with the implication that if man is to be God-like he must try in some measure to make these attributes his own. If God is described as righteous, truthful, faithful, upright and pure, man must endeavour to possess these qualities. However, Jewish thinkers have remarked that the doctrine of the Imitation of God is never applied to the sterner attributes of the Deity. 'Just as God is merciful be thou merciful' is the basis of the Rabbinic approach to ethics but nowhere do the Rabbis say or suggest: 'Just as God is described as girt with vengeance be thou vengeful.'

הַיּוֹם יִכָּתֵב

Upon This Day Shall be Written (R. 61-62 and S.169-170)

In this hymn Israel, described as 'the branch', is urged to rouse itself and make supplication for the soul before the 'face of Him who dwelleth on high.' The author, Joseph ben Isaac Ibn Abitur, a famed Talmudist (end of 10th century), was a member of a distinguished Spanish family and a pupil of Rabbi Moses of Babylon at Cordova. After Moses' death Ibn Abitur was a candidate for the position of Rabbi at Cordova but the Caliph favoured Rabbi Moses' son who on his appointment excommunicated his rival. Ibn Abitur was later offered the Cordova Rabbinate but with true dignity and nobility of character he declined the position, praising the merits of his teacher's son.

אִמְרוּ לֵאלֹהִים

Say Ye Unto God (R.64-66 and S.172-176)

An alphabetical acrostic by Meshullam ben Kalonymous describing the majesty and glory of God. Though God is 'high and exalted above the summitless heavens' yet 'He keepeth mercy to a thousand generations' and 'He inhabiteth eternity with him that is contrite.' The whole hymn is a magnificent commentary on the saying of the Talmudic Rabbi that in every passage of Scripture where the greatness of God is found there, too, is found His humility.

עַל יִשְׂרָאֵל

Over Israel (R.68-69 and S.178-179)

Another hymn by Meshullam ben Kalonymous in which the relationship between Israel and God is described. Various attributes of God (in alphabetical order) are said to be 'over Israel,' i.e. to afford Israel protection and to evoke Israel's sense of gratitude. In so many words, the poet says that the Chosen People idea means that Israel recognises the majesty of God and seeks to obey His will. In Zangwill's words the Chosen People is a Choosing People.

הָאַדֶּרֶת וְהָאֱמוּנָה

Majesty and Faithfulness (R.70-71 and S.181-182)

A hymn which speaks of God as 'the Life of worlds', i.e. He who gives life to all worlds and which speaks of His attributes in alphabetical order after the fashion of the liturgical poets. The hymn is found in the Kabbalistic work known as *Pirke Hekhaloth* (The Tracts of the Heavenly Halls) which deals with the Divine Chariot seen by the prophet Ezekiel. These tracts originated in the circle of early Jewish mystics (pre-10th century) known as the 'chariot riders'.

לָאֵל עוֹרֵךְ דִּין

Unto God Who Ordereth Judgment (R.77 and S.189)

A hymn of Meshullam ben Kalonymous describing God's attributes and deeds when He judges mankind. Each sentence begins with a letter of the alphabet from *Aleph* to *Tav*. God is described as 'He who revealeth deep things in judgment' and as 'He who searcheth hearts on the day of judgment' but it is not a merciless scrutiny. He 'forgiveth the people borne up by him in judgment' and He 'answereth his suppliants on the day of judgment.'

אַל תָּבֹא בְמִשְׁפָּט עִמָּנוּ

Enter Not Into Judgment With Us (R. 85 and S.207)

Reader and Congregation repeat these Scriptural verses, mainly adapted from the Psalms, all of which have the same theme—God's mercy in judgment.

שֹׁפֵט כָּל הָאָרֶץ

Thou Judge of All the Earth (R.86 and S.207-208)

This hymn by Solomon ben Abun of France (*d.* 1190) asks for God's pardon at the time of the morning prayer which takes the place of the morning sacrifice in the Temple.

מִי אֵל כָּמוֹךָ

Shield of Abraham (R.101 and S.231-232)

The first six sentences of this hymn begin with the first six letters of the alphabet in order, the last four sentences with the last four letters. Each sentence corresponds to one of the seven blessings of the *Yom Kippur Amidah*. The hymn is by the greatest of the mediaeval hymn writers, Eleazar Kalir. Although more than two hundred poems of Kalir are known, details of his life are veiled in obscurity. Even the age in which he flourished is not known with certainty but evidence seems to point to the 8th or 9th century. A feature of Kalir's poetry, its rhyming clauses, is seen in this hymn.

Torah Readings

An important part of the day's observance is the Torah reading. Reading from the Scroll of the Torah has occupied from ancient times a prominent place in public worship. The mystics, in particular, invest this part of the service with great solemnity, looking upon it as the re-enactment of the Revelation drama. The holier the day, the greater the number of persons called to the Torah. Thus, on an ordinary Monday or Thursday or on a minor fast-day, three people are called; on the New Moon, on Hannukah and Purim, four people; on the Festivals, five; on *Yom Kippur* morning, six, and on the Sabbath, seven. (In the traditional Jewish sources the Sabbath possesses an even greater degree of sanctity than *Yom Kippur*, though in the popular consciousness the latter has naturally been invested with a special sanctity which sets it apart from any other day in the Jewish year.)

The Torah Reading for the Morning (R.110-113 and S.244-249)

Two Scrolls are taken from the Ark. From the first the lengthy account of the ancient *Kippur* ritual in the Sanctuary (*Lev.* xvi) is read. The reading from the Second Scroll comes from the book of Numbers (xxix: 7-11) describing the sacrifices of the day. Both these *Torah* readings are chanted in the special, haunting, traditional tune for *Rosh Ha-Shanah* and *Yom Kippur*, expressive of yearning and longing for reconciliation, of confidence and hope in God's justice and mercy.

The Prophetic Reading (R.114-115 and S.249-252) The prophetic reading is from the book of Isaiah (lvii: 14 - lviii: 14). The prophet cannot abide his people's claim that they worship God in truth for he sees that they are engaged in oppression and practise injustice. The true worshipper of God will have charitable feelings. The fast which God has chosen is not one 'for strife and contention' in which a man bows his head in apparent submission to God while disregarding His word about charity and compassion. The fast which God chooses is one on which a man resolves to let the oppressed go free, to feed the hungry and clothe the naked. 'Then shall thy light rise in darkness, and thine obscurity as noonday.'

The historical background of these chapters is the Return from Exile after seventy years in Babylon. The prophet sees his people returning to the land of their fathers and admonishes them to practise justice and mercy so that their efforts will prosper and they will repair the land they loved which was laid in ruins.

הַזְכָּרַת נְשָׁמוֹת

Memorial Service for the Departed (R.118-120 and S.256-260)

The idea of praying for the souls of the departed is

ancient. In the second book of the Maccabees it is said that Judah collected the sum of two thousand drachmas of silver and sent it to Jerusalem as a sin offering for those who had died 'in that he was mindful of the resurrection. For if he had not hoped that they that were slain should have risen again, it had been superfluous and vain to pray for the dead. And also in that he perceived that there was great favour laid up for those that died godly, it was an holy and good thought. Whereupon he made a reconciliation for the dead, that they might be delivered from sin.'

That the living can atone by their charity for those who have died is found in a number of passages in the Rabbinic literature. Arising out of this belief it became customary to recite special prayers for the dead and to donate to charity on their behalf on *Yom Kippur*. At first these prayers were recited on *Yom Kippur* only (the Torah reading for *Yom Kippur* morning begins with the words: 'And the Lord spake unto Moses *after the death* of the two sons of Aaron . . .')

In the order of prayers known as *Mahzor Vitry* (1208) reference is made to memorial prayers on *Yom Kippur*, not on the other festivals. But at a later date the custom arose of reciting these prayers on all festival days on which the portion of the Torah dealing with the duty of supporting the poor is read, namely on the last days of Passover and Pentecost and on the eighth day of Tabernacles.

The central idea behind the Memorial Service is that a person's life does not come to an end with the death of his body. His soul lives on in two ways. First, Judaism teaches that the soul of man is immortal, that after his bodily death it continues to exist and that therefore what we do with our lives is of eternal significance. And secondly, the soul of a man who has influenced others lives on, here on earth, even when he has gone to his eternal rest. By remembering their parents in the Memorial Prayer, sons and daughters keep their memory alive by resolving to follow in their teachings.

וּנְתַנֶּה תֹּקֶף

Unethanneh Tokef (R.149-150 and S.ii, 32-34)

This is probably the best known of the *Yom Kippur* hymns describing how God sits on His throne of justice and writes down the fate of all His creatures on *Rosh Ha-Shanah* sealing the decree of *Yom Kippur*. The hymn concludes that 'Repentance, Prayer and Charity have the power of averting the evil decree.'

The hymn was composed by Meshullam ben Kalonymous, the author of many of the *Yom Kippur* hymns. Legend has it that the prayer was really composed by Rabbi Amnon of Mayence who, after his death, revealed it to Meshullam in a dream. According to this legend, Amnon resisted all the efforts of the Archbishop of Mayence to have him converted to Christianity. The Rabbi was tortured and his hands and feet cut off. As he was about to die he asked to be carried into the Synagogue. It was *Yom Kippur* and the Congregation were about to recite the *Kedushah* prayer, the prayer of Sanctification of God's name. Rabbi Amnon recited the *Unethanneh Tokef* prayer, then expired. Most scholars, however, argue from the style and language of the meditation that, in fact, it originated at a much earlier date and that Meshullam simply added the final touches.

While there is a certain grandeur about the meditation and while its popularity has been attested to throughout the ages it cannot be denied that if taken too literally the hymn can be offensive to modern tastes. Particularly the suggestion of repentance, prayer and charity as means of averting the divine threat of a horrible death 'by fire, by water, by the sword, by wild beasts, by earthquake, by plague, by strangling and by stoning' is hardly likely to prove the best incentive to the living of the good life. The problem of pain, the mystery of why the good God allows evil to exist, is one that has exercised the minds of the greatest religious thinkers. Various solutions have been offered but when all is said we have to confess defeat. We have to recognise that we are in the presence of the unfathomable, that the finite mind of man cannot hope to penetrate the secrets of the Infinite. But our faith insists on the belief in the goodness of God.

וְכֹל מַאֲמִינִים

And All Believe (R.152-154 and S.ii, 39-41)

This hymn of early origin begins each half-line with a letter of the alphabet from *Aleph* to *Tav*, but each alternate line has the words *vekhol maaminim shehu* (and all believe that He is) before the word beginning with the appropriate letter. The word *maaminim* is from the same root as the word *Amen*. Its meaning is trust, faith, conviction, affirmation. The Hebrew word for faith is *Emunah*, for the man of faith=*Maamin*, of which *maaminim* is the plural.

וְיֶאֱתָיוּ כֹּל לְעָבְדֶךָ

And All the World Shall Come (R.154-155 and S.ii, 43)

Another alphabetical hymn describing the universalistic hopes of Judaism that the day will come when men will cast away their idols and all men will worship God in truth. This, too, is a very early hymn of uncertain origin. Zunz considers the author to be Eleazar Kalir.

עָלֵינוּ

Alenu (R.157 and S.ii, 48)

This ancient, sublime prayer, describing Israel's longing for the establishment of the kingdom of Heaven on earth, originally belonged to the special New Year *Amidah* whence it was taken to conclude every Jewish service. On *Rosh Ha-Shanah* and *Yom Kippur* the whole congregation falls to the ground at the words: 'we bend the knee and prostrate ourselves and make acknowledgment before the supreme King of kings.' Tradition has it that the prayer was composed by Joshua on entering Palestine but the generally accepted view is that Rab, the famous second-century teacher, introduced it into his arrangement of the *Rosh Ha-Shanah Amidah*. This is not to say that Rab was its composer. From such evidence as the use of the term 'King of kings' some scholars conclude that the hymn dates back to the Persian period (539-331 B.C.E.).

The verse: 'For they prostrate themselves before vanity and folly, and pray to a god which cannot help' was excised by the Christian censors on the grounds that it referred to Jesus. This is historically incorrect, for the prayer is probably pre-Christian or in any event composed in Jewish circles where Christians were virtually unknown. The result of these accusations against the Alenu prayer has been the omission of the above-mentioned phrase and the mutilation of other parts of the prayer.

Dr. Hertz, in his lengthy note on *Alenu* in his commentary to the Prayer Book, quotes the remarks of Manasseh ben Israel in his *Vindiciae Judaeorum* that the Sultan Selim on reading the prayer for the first time in a Turkish translation said: 'Truly this prayer is sufficient for all purposes; there is no need of any other.'

אֱלֹהֵינוּ וֵאלֹהֵי אֲבוֹתֵינוּ

Our God and God of Our Fathers (R.158 and S.ii, 49-51)

This is the supplication of the Reader before he begins the *Abhodah*, the portion of the *Amidah* describing the Temple service on *Yom Kippur*.

עֲבוֹדָה

Abhodah (R.159-165 and S.ii, 52-61)

The *Abhodah* (service, Temple worship) is the order of worship of the Israelites in the Temple. It is related during the *Yom Kippur Musaph* service in order to recall former glories and to re-enact symbolically the ancient rites. The descriptive verses by Meshullam ben Kalonymous are based on the Talmudic accounts.

The first paragraph of the *Abhodah* speaks of God creating all things, of the creation of Adam and Eve, of their sin, of Cain and Abel, of Noah, Abraham, Isaac and Jacob, of Jacob's son, Levi, from whom the High Priest, the hero of the day, was descended. Then begins the account of the preparations for the great day of worship and of the service itself.

The High Priest made confession three times—once for himself, once for his household and the priests, and once for all the congregation of Israel. When making these confessions he would pronounce the 'glorious and awful name,' i.e. the ineffable name of God which could not be pronounced at any other time and when the people and the priests heard it they fell upon their faces. When the Reader and congregation refer to the priests and the people prostrating themselves (R.161–162 and 164) they, too, fall to the ground on their knees and touch the ground with their faces. The account concludes with the prayer the High Priest recited when he came forth in safety from the Holy of Holies (the tradition has it that if the High Priest were unworthy he would not survive his entry into the sacred spot on such a day). The prayer ends with the plea that the houses of the inhabitants of the plain of Sharon, built on shifting sands, may not become their graves.

מַרְאֵה כֹהֵן

As the Brightness (R.166–167 and S.ii, 62)

This is by an unknown author but is based on the fiftieth chapter of the book of Ecclesiasticus in which is described the appearance of the High Priest, Simon, when he came out of the Sanctuary.

אַשְׁרֵי עַיִן

Happy the Eye (R.167–168 and S.ii, 62–63)

The service continues with the lament that all the glories have departed and that we can no longer witness such scenes. This lament begins with the hymn of Solomon Ibn Gabirol (*c.*1021–*c.*1058), the distinguished Spanish philosopher and poet, each line of which begins with the refrain: 'Happy the eye that saw.'

אֲנִי הוּא הַשּׁוֹאֵל

I am the Suppliant (R.172-174 and S.ii, 277-279)

This rhyming hymn was composed by Baruch ben Samuel (*d.* 1221) of Mayence. Baruch ben Samuel was the author of the well-known Sabbath table hymn, '*Baruch El Elyon*,' the first word of which is his own name.

אִם יוֹסְפִים אֲנַחְנוּ

Since We be Standing (R.175-176 and S.ii, 80-81)

This hymn was composed by Ephraim ben Isaac of Regensburg (*d.* 1175). Ephraim was a renowned Talmudist as well as liturgical poet and is said to have introduced the use of the spice-box for the Habhdalah ceremony.

אֵלֶּה אֶזְכְּרָה

These Things I do Remember (R.178-181 and S.ii, 85-89)

The Roman Emperor Hadrian, resolved to stamp out Judaism ruthlessly, engaged on a bloody persecution during which many of Israel's sages perished. In those days numerous Jewish families gave their lives for the Sabbath, circumcision and other Jewish institutions. Tradition records that ten great sages were slain during the Hadrianic persecutions. Later legend describes how they were all killed on the same day, though this is historically incorrect. This dirge in the *Yom Kippur* liturgy is based on a late Midrash and describes the martyrdom of the ten sages in detail.

No mention is made here of the Hadrianic persecutions. Instead it is said that the Emperor, after reading in the Torah the account of Joseph and his brothers, asked the Sages the punishment for one who steals a man. When they answered that he was to be sentenced to death the Emperor ordered them to be put to death to expiate the sin of Joseph's brothers, their ancestors. Ishmael inquired in Heaven if this were indeed to be their fate and he was told that they must be prepared to die. The theology of the dirge is inconsistent with the general Jewish view that descendants do not suffer for the sins of their ancestors. Because of this difficulty and the anachronisms in the dirge Dr. H. J. Zimmels is of the opinion that the whole lament is a veiled attack on the Church which persecuted the Jews.

Among the ten martyrs were Akiba who died with a smile on his lips in obedience to the verse: 'And thou shalt love thy God with all thy life' which Akiba interpreted to mean: 'Even if thy life is demanded,' and Hananiah ben Teradion who was burned at the stake with a Sefer Torah wrapped round his body and who said that he saw 'the parchments burning but the letters of the Torah flying aloft.'

CHAPTER 6

THE AFTERNOON AND NEILAH PRAYERS

The Afternoon Service (R.197-242 and S.ii, 113-179)

The Afternoon Torah Reading (R.199-200 and S.ii, 116-119)

The afternoon reading is the account of the forbidden marriages in the eighteenth chapter of the book of Leviticus. This choice of reading has been variously explained—as a reminder of the importance of loyalty to the Jewish ideals and lofty standards of family life or a warning of the dangers of temptation. But the more probable reason is that, as the sixteenth chapter of Leviticus is read in the morning, the eighteenth chapter of the same book was a natural choice for the afternoon reading. (The seventeenth chapter deals chiefly with the laws concerning the slaughter of animals 'outside the camp' which have no relevance to Jewish life after the destruction of the Temple.)

The chapter opens with the injunction: 'Ye shall therefore keep my statutes, and my judgments; which if a man do, he shall live in them,' on which the Rabbis comment 'live in them' and not 'die in them.' That is to say the Torah is a 'Torah of life.' Its aim is to promote healthy, worthwhile, noble living.

The Book of Jonah (R.201-204 and S.ii, 119-124)

As the afternoon prophetic portion the whole of the book of Jonah is read, with the addition of the three verses from the book of Micah (vii: 18-20) describing God's mercy. The lessons of the book of Jonah—that God takes pity on all His creatures, that He is the God of all men ready to accept the repentance of those who turn to Him in truth, that it is impossible to fly from the Presence of God—make it an obvious choice for *Yom Kippur* reading.

Jonah, the prophet of the Lord, knew, the Midrash remarks, that God is everywhere, that you cannot fly from Him in space. What, then, was the purpose of the prophet's flight to Tarshish? Jonah knew, answers the Midrash, that the Divine Presence can rest on the prophet only in the Holy Land, so that by escaping to a land where there was no holiness, by deliberately submitting to an inferior way of life and thus forfeiting the right to see the prophetic vision, he thought to evade the tremendous responsibility that is part of the prophet's burden.

The Opening Prayers (R.215-218 and S.ii, 138-142)

The opening prayers tell of the faithfulness of Abraham and the song of the angels to whom Israel is compared on *Yom Kippur*. These hymns were composed by Elijah ben Mordecai (11th century).

מַשְׂאַת כַּפַּי מִנְחַת עֶרֶב

The Lifting of Mine Hands Accept (R.224-226 and S.ii, 152-154)

It is a well-known Rabbinic doctrine that the daily services correspond to the twice-daily offerings in the Temple. The *Minhah* service corresponds to the Afternoon offering and on this correspondence the hymn is based. This hymn was composed by the thirteenth-century liturgical poet, Mordecai ben Shabbethai who lived either in Greece or Italy and who was known as 'Mordecai The Tall'.

לְךָ יְיָ הַצְּדָקָה תִּלְבֹּשֶׁת

O Lord Thou Art Clothed in Righteousness (R.226-227 and S.ii, 156-158)

The refrain of this hymn composed by Solomon ben Judah Hababli (11th century) is an adaptation of the plea of Miriam and Aaron to be forgiven for slandering Moses: 'Oh my Lord, lay not, I pray thee, sin upon us, for that we have done foolishly, and for that we have sinned.' (*Num.* xii: 11).

אֱמוּנִים בְּנֵי מַאֲמִינִים

Faithful Sons of Faithful Sires (R.228-229 and S.ii, 159-161)

This descriptive hymn of the Binding of Isaac was composed by the eleventh-century poet, Benjamin ben Zerah, known as the 'Master of the Name' because of his use of the divine names in many of his poems.

נְעִילָה

Neilah

In Temple times deputations of laymen were delegated to be present each day when the priests offered up the sacrifices on behalf of Israel. Towards the end of the day when the Temple gates were about to be shut these men would recite the Prayer of the Closing of the Gates (*Neilath Shearim—Neilah*='to close'). On fast days this special concluding service was added to the prayers of the day but in the course of time this addition was reserved for *Yom Kippur*. At a later period it was natural to associate the idea of the closing gates with the gates of Heaven open to prayer during the long day. The note sounded at *Neilah* is one of hope. The sun is about to set, the prayers have ascended on high, Israel has become reconciled to its God. The traditional melodies express the mood of longing, of yearning for a better life, of triumph over sin.

The Neilah Amidah (R.246-252 and S.ii, 183-191)

The special feature of the *Neilah Amidah* is the prayer 'Thou givest the hand to transgressors' (pp. 250-251). God is described as ready to forgive, man as insignificant before His majesty. Twice the phrase occurs 'so that we may stay our hands from oppression' for, as we have noted, it is offences against one's neighbour for which even *Yom Kippur* cannot atone unless adequate restitution is made. Jewish moralists advise that when this prayer is recited the worshipper make a firm resolve to put right any wrongs he has committed against his fellows.

In this prayer, as in so many others of the day, two contrasting views of man are stated. On the one hand man is insignificant, on the other he is of great significance. 'Are not all the mighty ones as naught before thee, and the men of fame as though they were not, wise men as if they were without knowledge, and men of understanding as though they were devoid of discretion? For the multitude of their works is emptiness, and the days of their life are vanity before thee; and the pre-eminence of man over beast is naught: for all is vanity.' Yet in the very next paragraph the prayer goes on to say: 'Thou hast set man apart from the beginning and acknowledged him that he should stand before thee.' For, rightly understood, puny, insignificant man on his tiny planet whirling through space is of supreme significance for he can recognise God and do His will.

זְכוֹר בְּרִית אַבְרָהָם

Remember The Covenant of Abraham (R.262 and S.ii, 203-204)

The author of this hymn of supplication was Gershom bar Judah (*b.* Metz, 960) known as 'The Light of the Exile.' Rabenu Gershom was the foremost teacher of German Jewry in the eleventh century. At a famous Synod summoned by him round about the year 1,000 a number of far-reaching enactments were made. Among these were two which had as their aim the amelioration of the lot of the Jewish woman—that she could not be divorced by her husband without her consent and that polygamy was to be outlawed.

אֶזְכְּרָה אֱלֹהִים וְאֶהֱמָיָה

Lord, I Remember (R.263 and S.ii, 205)

A hymn of supplication by Amittai ben Shephatiah (11th century) based on the thirteen attributes of mercy. A number of Rabbinic authorities objected to the original reading of the second verse of this hymn in which the divine quality of mercy was personified and entreated to 'crave compassion for thy people's sake.' Traditional Judaism knows of no intermediary between man and his Maker. In the Routledge Prayer Book the verse has been altered to preserve the rhyme and rhythm of the original without its grounds for offence. Amittai ben Shephatiah lived in Italy about 900 and was one of the first liturgical poets in Europe.

Sealing in the Book of Life

The Rabbis speak of the books of life and death, open during the ten days from *Rosh Ha-Shanah* to *Yom Kippur*. Towards the end of *Kippur* man's fate is sealed. Hence the many references to 'sealing in the book of life' during the *Neilah* prayers. But as Israel Abrahams remarks: 'this must not be interpreted too literally; that the gate of repentance is always open is a truth inculcated by the Rabbis in scores of passages.'

שְׁמַע יִשְׂרָאֵל

Hear, O Israel (R.271 and S.ii, 215)

The *Neilah* Service concludes with the recitation of the *Shema*, of Blessed be his glorious Name, and of the words uttered by Israel on Mount Carmel when they saw the hand of God: 'The Lord he is God.' At first only the last verse was recited seven times. At a later date the other two verses were added.

The Blowing of the Shofar

Among the reasons given for the custom of blowing the Shofar at the end of *Yom Kippur* are that it is a reminder of the Jubilee year on which slaves were set free which began on the Tenth Day of Tishri and which was announced by the Shofar, and that it is to mark the end of the fast day. It does not require much imagination to read into it the idea of sounding the note of confidence and hope and triumph over sin.

CHAPTER 7

THE CONFESSION OF SIN

Confession

The value of confession is obvious. The wrongdoer feels a pressing need not alone to make good the wrongs he has done but to express contrition. The Rabbis teach that confession of sin is an integral part of true repentance. They disapproved of confessing sins to a human being. God alone was to be the recipient of admissions of human failure. True, here and there in the moralistic literature, especially among the mediaeval mystics known as the Hasidim of Ashkenaz, we find the advice given to confess one's shortcomings to a trusted friend but, on the whole, it is safe to say that Judaism has nothing corresponding to the idea of confession to a priest with powers of absolution.

Originally there was no fixed formula of confession. Each person on *Yom Kippur* confessed to any sins he had committed during the past year. In the course of time two fixed formulas were adopted—*Ashamnu* and *Al Het*. The alphabetical acrostic form of these two confessions has puzzled many. Does this not reduce the whole of the confession to a purely mechanical act devoid of inwardness? The usual answer is that in the days before the invention of printing such devices were essential if the prayers were to be remembered. There is, too, much point in the observation that where the congregation adopts the same form of confession the individual is spared embarrassment if his confession is overheard. In Temple times, the Rabbis teach, the sin offering was slaughtered in the same place as other offerings in order not to put the sinner to shame.

Another difficulty mentioned in a number of sources is what should a man do if he is sure that he has never in his life been guilty of some of the offences enumerated in the two formal confessions? Many teachers refer in this connection to the doctrine that each Israelite is responsible for the sins of his fellows. Though the idea of collective responsibility can be over-stressed there is much in the thought that the good man sets an example of goodness while the wrongdoer lowers the standard and makes it more difficult for others to do the right thing.

There is, too, the idea that for the greater man a minor sin is comparable to a major transgression of a lesser person for the greater man ought to know better. This is behind such Rabbinic teaching as that he who flies into a rage is as one who worships idols. Seen in this light the whole list of sins is applicable to each one, for even where a man is not guilty of infringement in a gross sense he may be held culpable for a sin akin to the original prohibition.

Ashamnu (R.i: pp. 7, 26, 46; ii, pp. 49, 93, 130, 184, 211, 233, 250 and 264; S.i.: pp. 25, 51, 152, 222; ii: pp. 9, 93, 132, 166, 188, 206).

The exact origin of this older form of the confession (called the 'shorter' confession in contrast to the 'longer,' *Al Het*) is unknown but is very early. There is a reference to it as long ago as two thousand years. The custom of beating the breast when reciting this (and the *Al Het*) confession symbolises that sin originates in the heart.

Al Het (R.i: pp. 8-10, 26-28, 49-51; ii, pp. 49-51, 96-98, 130-133, 211-214; S.i; pp. 26-29, 54-57, 153-156, 225-228; ii: pp. 10-13, 96-99, 133-136, 169-172)

The *Al Het* form of confession has grown gradually from a list of six sins to the present catalogue in which each letter of the alphabet is used for two sins. The point has often been made that the list embraces chiefly ethical offences rather than ritual ones. The following are brief comments on the clauses of *Al Het* which require elucidation. There are a number of apparent repetitions in this formula, possibly due to the need for preserving the alphabetical acrostic.

Under Compulsion or of Freewill

A man can only be held responsible for the sins he could have avoided. An offence committed under duress, the Rabbis rightly teach, is no sin. What, then, is the meaning of 'under compulsion'? Two explanations have been given.

1 That Jewish law demands, on occasion, that a man sacrifice his life for his faith, i.e. in times of religious persecution. On such occasions even a sin committed under duress is held to be culpable.

2 Though a sick person, ordered to do so by his physician, may eat forbidden food or profane the Sabbath, he should do so with regret.

By Hardening of the Heart

This means both hardening the heart against the plea of the needy or the calls on compassion, and deadening the conscience so that it fails to disturb. An over-sensitive conscience can make a man's life a misery but some degree of sensitivity of conscience is basic to a healthy religious outlook.

Unwittingly

Even a sin committed unwittingly is accounted a sin if it could have been prevented. This covers the harm done by the thoughtless, the tactlessness which wounds, failure to recognise the way in which help can be extended to others, ignorance of Jewish teaching through carelessness or indifference. Another interpretation of the Hebrew *Bibhli Daath* is 'without understanding,' i.e. the sin for which there is no rhyme nor reason, the sin from which no one benefits.

Openly and Secretly

The thief who steals openly, said R. Johanan ben Zakkai, and thus defies the laws of both God and man, is like the man who invites neither the king nor the people to his banquet. But the thief who steals at night in secret, defying God's law but fearful of man's, is like he who invites the people and fails to invite the king. His offence is the greater. But this distinction applies to ethical offences only (for here the offence is against both God and man). With regard to religious offences, brazen defiance is far worse than succumbing to temptation when no one knows, i.e. the open profanation of the Sabbath is the greater offence than its desecration in secret.

Knowingly and Deceitfully

i.e. where the victim knows that he has been wronged and where he has been defrauded without his knowledge. Or this may mean: where a man knows that he has done wrong and where he deludes himself into thinking that no harm has been done. Or the meaning may be: both where he defies the law and where he tries to discover loopholes within it.

In the Meditation of the Heart

The Rabbis teach that though a man is not held culpable for sinful thoughts, these have the effect, nonetheless, of contaminating the heart and bringing about sin.

Wronging a Neighbour

This includes what the Rabbis meant when they spoke of wronging with words, i.e. to remind a convert to Judaism that his ancestors worshipped false gods or to remind a repentant sinner of his former life or to suggest to a man who suffers that his affliction is due to sin.

Confession of the Lips

This can mean either public confession which, as we have seen, is frowned upon in Judaism or confession with the lips alone without the heart being involved.

Profanation of the Name

According to Rabbinic teaching this includes any act which, though not wrong in itself, results in disrespect for the Torah and its teachings. As Israel Salanter, the famous 19th-century moralist, put it: 'I know that I am neither very pious nor a great scholar but because people mistakenly think I am both it is my duty to be absolutely above suspicion of any kind.' On the lower level, any act which causes the non-Jew to think poorly of the Jewish Community is a profanation of the divine Name.

By the Evil Inclination

But is not all sin the effect of the evil inclination? The meaning may be either by protesting that when we sin we are the victims of the evil inclination and not to blame, or wilful surrender to impulse as when a man 'works himself up into a frenzy.'

By Bribery

Not alone the bribes accepted by a judge but allowing ourselves to become motivated by bias and prejudice and refusing to give others a fair hearing. This condemns, too, the sycophant and the flatterer who allow their judgment to be clouded through love of gain.

Denying and Lying

Kahash is the denial of the truth, *Kazabh* is the failure to keep one's word.

Evil Speech

This refers specifically to slander. According to Rabbinic teaching it is forbidden to speak evil of another, even if what is said is true. Scripture, they say, compares slander to an arrow, not a sword, for when the sword wounds he who inflicts the wound can be seen but slander destroys without the victim knowing who is to blame.

Eating and Drinking

This includes the failure to observe Kashruth, gluttony, lack of care in diet to the detriment of one's health and the omission of saying grace. The table of man is his altar, is a well-known Rabbinic saying.

Usury and Increase

According to Rabbinic teaching, both these offences are one but usury refers to the amount the borrower loses, increase to the amount the lender gains.

Utterances of Our Lips

A repetition to preserve the acrostic. Or the meaning may be that we have prayed without inwardness.

Prayer without inwardness, the Jewish saying goes, is like a body without a soul.

Obdurate Brow

This refers to the brazen attitude which shews complete disregard of the opinion of others. As one of the commentaries to the Prayer Book remarks, the man of 'obdurate *brow*' tries to compensate for his deficiency of *inner* strength of character by pretending to an artificial strength that is merely external.

Breaking Off the Yoke

The good man has many responsibilities—to his wife and family, to his people, to his faith, to his house of worship, to charitable causes, to himself. These are the yoke he must bear. 'Breaking off the yoke' is to act irresponsibly as if these obligations did not exist.

Envy

Envy is, according to the Rabbis, one of the three things which 'take a man out of the world.' Many a man's life is soured because he cannot bear to witness the successes of others. The Hebrew literally means 'narrowness of eye' and includes miserliness and lack of charity.

Running to do Evil

i.e. not only did we sin, we *ran* to the sin, we took delight in it.

Causeless Hatred

But there is always a cause for hatred? No, said one of

the Hasidic teachers, for sometimes the hatred is not caused by the 'cause', the 'cause' is 'caused' by the hatred. Jerusalem was destroyed because of causeless hatred, say the Rabbis. The late Rabbi Kook, the Chief Rabbi of Palestine, was rebuked by a zealot for showing affection to anti-religious people. Jerusalem was destroyed, he replied, by those who practised causeless hatred; it can only be rebuilt by those who practise *causeless* love.

Breach of Trust

The Hebrew term includes acting as a harsh creditor and refusing to lend to others.

Terror of the Heart

This includes unreasonable fears and superstitions and the lack of faith which leaves a man without anchorage in his life. 'The atheist is the man who has no invisible means of support.'

And for the Sins

The confession ends with a list of the sins for which various penalties were meted out in Temple times. Scholars have pointed out that, in fact, the 'four death penalties' were hardly ever carried out in practice, the Rabbis preventing their literal application by every kind of restriction. Rabbi Akiba said that had he have been on the Sanhedryn the death penalty would never have been carried out.

The long confession begins with: 'Thou knowest the

mysteries of the Universe and the secrets of all living.' The Talmud states that this was the prayer of Rab (*d.* 247). It concludes with: 'O my God, before I was formed I was nothing worth . . . ' attributed in one Talmudic passage to R. Hamnuna (4th century), in another passage it is said that Raba (*d.* 352) would conclude his daily prayer with these words. Israel Abrahams suggests that the teachers mentioned may not have composed these prayers but adopted them as part of their order of service.

CHAPTER 8

SIN

The Reality of Sin

At the beginning of the *Yom Kippur* service the whole congregation repeats three times after the Reader the verse, from the narrative in the Book of Numbers describing how God heard Moses' plea for mercy when his people had sinned: 'And the Lord said: "I have pardoned according to thy word." ' The verse contains three significant ideas upon which the observance of *Yom Kippur* is based. 1. *That sin is real, an offence against God;* 2. *That God, nonetheless, pardons sin;* 3. *That such pardon must be bought by man's efforts*—'according to thy word.'

That sin is real is basic to *Yom Kippur*. Unless we can be said to sin and to require forgiveness there can be no meaning in the idea of atonement. Many people, particularly at the end of the last century and the beginning of this, were prepared to challenge the proposition that sin is real. They would have said that the whole concept of sin is out-dated. Man, in this view, never sins. He is not to blame for his faults, for his failure to do right, for his persistence in doing wrong. All the mistakes a man makes, all the man-made evils by which the face of humanity is blackened, are due to faulty upbringing, to inadequate training on the part of stupid parents and teachers, to an unsound economy, a bad society, an unfortunate environment or to psychological maladjustment. The bad man is the victim of circumstance. Society must take steps to protect itself against his designs but he is no more to *blame* for what he is than the man afflicted with bodily disease. In this view, all talk of atonement is obsolete. What man needs is the removal of evils external to himself. Only allow men to live in a good society, only provide children with sound educational programmes, only permit the psychologist to do his job effectively and sin will be no more. There is no propensity for evil in the human soul.

One of the most significant advances of our time is the recognition that given better social conditions in which to flourish men will become better. We recognise today the value of penal reform with its aim of reclaiming the criminal instead of destroying him. We see the need for psychological treatment for the mentally disturbed and unbalanced. We appreciate how important it is to provide children with a good home background and to use sound pedagogical methods in their education and training. But it is to take an exceedingly superficial view of human nature to imagine that all man's problems are external to him. 'The heart of man is evil from his youth' the Bible teaches, which means that social reforms, highly important though they are, will fail of their aim unless they are accompanied by the reform which begins in the heart. We of this generation know the truth of this for we have seen evil. We know of the depths to which human nature can sink.

It might with justice be argued that the evils we have

witnessed in our generation are examples of irrationality run riot. That a Hitler was a monster of evil whose behaviour has nothing whatever to do with that of normal people. That we must not attempt to deduce the character of man from the bestial and sub-human. There is much point to the objection and yet a great question mark has been added during the past three decades to Victorian optimism about man and his nature. We cannot help asking: if *any* man can sink to such depths does this not taint and render suspect the character of *every* man? And in moments of honesty do we not recognise the 'evil inclination' in ourselves? Do we not know of the wrongs we have done to others, including those we love? Of the standards we have set ourselves from which we have fallen short? Of the good we have thrown away and the evil we have embraced? And in such moments we know that with all the extenuating circumstances and with all the excuses we are ready to find for ourselves, we are to blame and we want to shoulder the blame rather than lay it at another's door.

Sin is real. But nowadays this is so well realised that the tendency is to overlook man's potentialities for good by dwelling on his depravity. If we can no longer accept the facile view that man is an angel, there is no reason for going to the opposite extreme of seeing him as a devil. The attitudes of Judaism and Christianity have frequently been contrasted. Christianity it is said believes in the doctrine of Original Sin, that all men are born tainted with sin as the result of the Fall. Judaism, it is said, does not know of this doctrine. Judaism, in

Zangwill's words, is a 'cheery faith.' This distinction, however, is far too simple. It would not be difficult to shew that in Judaism, too, there are echoes of the Original Sin idea and the Biblical view of man certainly does not lend itself to an over-confident and superficially optimistic outlook on man's virtuous possibilities. But there is a marked difference in emphasis between the two faiths in this matter. It has been said that Christianity teaches that man sins because he is a sinner while Judaism teaches that he is a sinner because he sins! Allowing for the inevitable distortions and simplifications of generalisation there is much truth in this. In traditional Judaism there is no doctrine of despair of man, sapping his confidence in himself and in his power for good. Judaism sees no need for a saviour to redeem man from sin. Man redeems himself with the help of God.

This is the Jewish outlook expressed in many of the *Yom Kippur* prayers. *Sin is real but man can conquer sin.* Judaism insists that we can control our lives. That we are not, to use the illustration given by a well-known Jewish preacher, like the train in Zola's novel, the driver of which is struck dead at the throttle of his locomotive, leaving his train to go roaring madly through the night.

There are, naturally, in the Jewish sources teachings which remind man of his lowliness that, as a second century teacher puts it, he goes to a place of dust, worms and maggots. But the opposite view, which dwells on man's exalted state as a being created in God's image, is found in many pages of Jewish religious literature.

Judaism teaches that if man has an evil inclination he has a good inclination, too. God helps him to fight the evil in himself and in the world. Right at the beginning of the Bible Cain is told: 'Sin coucheth at the door, and unto thee is its desire, but thou mayest rule over it.'

The Categories of Sin

In Biblical Hebrew there are three main terms for sin—*pesha*, *avon* and *het*. These express different categories of sin, though the distinctions are not always adhered to, especially in the later literature. In the *Yom Kippur* liturgy, for instance, the word most frequently used for sin is *het* and it is used apparently for every kind of sinfulness. But originally the terms had the following meanings:

Pesha means rebellion. It refers to the attitude of mind through which a man sets himself up as the sole judge of his actions, recognising neither God nor His law. *Pesha* signifies the refusal of man to consider himself accountable to God for his actions. For this type of man there are no external standards of right and wrong. Right is the name he gives to those actions which please him and further his aims, wrong, to those which displease him and frustrate his aims.

Avon comes from a root meaning 'to be twisted,' 'to be crooked.' It refers to the man whose course in life is deflected from the pursuit of the good (compare our slang word 'a crook'). It refers also to the twist in a man's character which seems to impel him to do wrong, to a queer perversity of temperament which propels him in the direction of wrong-doing. How often does it happen that a highly gifted man with brilliant opportunities throws everything away in an act of folly!

Het is the weakest of the three terms. It comes from a root meaning 'to miss.' The word is used, for example of an archer whose arrows fail to hit the target. *Het* denotes failure to follow the good path, to the lack of character or staying power which prevents a man from arriving at the goal he has set himself. The Rabbinic term *shogeg*, meaning unwitting sin, roughly corresponds to the term *het*. Blame is attached even to unwitting sin if it could have been avoided with the exercise of greater care. The careless driver, the slack teacher, the over-indulgent or the neglectful parent, the thoughtless son, are all guilty of *het*.

The Rabbis generally speak of sin as *Abherah* (in opposition to the *mitzvah*, the good deed, from a root meaning 'to command,' i.e. the good deed is a divine command). *Abherah* is derived from a root meaning 'to pass over,' i.e. sin is passing over the line of rectitude, it is a transgression against God's laws. In the Bible story of Adam and Eve God says 'Do not eat of the fruit of the tree' and they say: 'We will eat.' For that is what sin means, saying: 'I will' when God has said 'Do not.'

CHAPTER 9

REPENTANCE

Repentance

Teshubah, the Hebrew word for repentance, means 'turning back.' Man has become estranged from God as a result of his sins. By resolving to change his ways he becomes reconciled with his Maker.

> *Seek ye the Lord while He may be found,*
> *Call ye upon Him while He is near;*
> *Let the wicked forsake his way,*
> *And the man of iniquity his thoughts;*
> *And let him return unto the Lord, and*
> *He will have compassion upon him,*
> *And to our God, for He will abundantly pardon*
> (Isaiah, lv: 6-7).

Sin is conceived of in Jewish literature as a barrier between man and God. Repentance enables a man to break through that barrier or to remove it entirely. The eighteenth-century poet, mystic and moralist, Moses Hayyim Luzzatto (1707-1747) compares the divine love to the rays of the sun which can only penetrate into a room if the windows are clean. By repentance man cleans the windows of his soul to allow the divine light to enter. We are, of course, using here pictorial language. But the idea expressed is known to us from the depths of our own experience. There are times when God is very real to us, others when He is remote. Man cannot be near to God when defying His will. 'While He may be found' is applied by the Rabbis to the ten days from *Rosh Ha-Shanah* to *Yom Kippur*. For during these days of self-examination and self-improvement the barriers are removed and man is near to God.

The Jewish ideal is not fusion with God but nearness to Him. 'But as for me, the nearness of God is my good,' sings the Psalmist. 'They delight to draw near to God,' says Isaiah. This is what repentance means. That man should seek God and return to the path leading to Him whenever he has strayed from it. The early Hasidic teachers used the bold imagery of the father who pretends to hide from his little boy in order to increase the child's delight on finding him. God is hidden, they say, but for the man who knows that He is hidden and sincerely tries to find Him He is not truly hidden. This is why so much importance is attached in Judaism to the *deed*. Man eventually finds God through constant practice and persistence in doing right actions. The *Shema* speaks, said the Rabbi of Kotzk (*d.* 1859), of the word of God being '*upon* thine heart,' not '*in* thine heart.' For who can say that the word of God is always in his heart? But by persisting in the way of the Torah, even if, at times, it all seems hopelessly remote, man is brought into permanent contact with spiritual things. When the word of God is constantly *upon* the heart it will often penetrate into the heart!

Repentance is then an affair of the heart. It implies, teach the Rabbis, two things—contrition for the sin committed and firm resolve not to repeat it. There have been Jews, particularly among the sect known as the Hasidim of Ashkenaz who flourished in mediaeval Germany (influenced in their practices, scholars say, by the Christian notions of self-mortification current at the time) who considered self-torment of one kind or another to be essential to the act of contrition.

But these practices are certainly the exception. Later Rabbinic authorities were opposed to them. What is demanded, these latter taught, was the sincere inner desire to repent. The great Maimonides gives as the test of sincere repentance that He who knows the secret things of the heart can testify that the sinner's remorse is so authentic that he will never again 'revert to folly.' Ezekiel Landau of Prague (1713-1793) whose decisions in matters of Jewish law still enjoy great authority, was approached by a scholar, who had committed many sins, for a penance. Landau urged the man to refrain from self-torture which would only deter him from his studies. The way a scholar repents, taught this famous Jew, is by devoting more time and energy to the study of the Torah.

Repentance from Fear and Repentance from Love

The Rabbis drew a distinction between two kinds of repentance. Repentance from fear of the consequences of sin is acceptable to God but is far removed from the highest form of repentance. The ideal is repentance out of love.

Religious people have sometimes placed far too much emphasis on the negative aspects of religion, on the struggle with evil, on the consequence of sin. But there is that other aspect of religion where man worships because he can do no other. The great Jews looked upon the Torah not as an irksome discipline or obedience to its demands as service at the treadmill but as an exhilarating way of life providing its adherents with true inner freedom, lifting them 'on eagles' wings' into the realms of the ideal. Struggling with the evil within is but one side of the religious life. 'Turn from evil and do good' was interpreted by a Hasidic saint to mean that the best way of overcoming evil is not to dwell morbidly on it but to transcend it in the doing of the good.

It may be asked, if this is correct why, then, so much emphasis on sin in the *Yom Kippur* liturgy? Why the long recitations of offences committed? The answer would appear to be that Judaism believes that man is on the side of goodness. That he is anxious to do the right thing and does not need to be told what good he should do, but rather what he should avoid doing. Concentration on the negative prohibitions, far from being evidence of a belief in man's depravity, is a conviction of his basic goodness. The Jew on *Yom Kippur* when he confesses to the wrongs he has done implies that these are departures from the norm. That 'God created man upright.'

Rabbinic Teachings on Repentance

Repentance is great, say the Rabbis, for it reaches to the very Throne of God, as it is said: 'Return, O Israel, unto the Lord thy God.' (*Hosea* xiv: 2) This verse is also interpreted to mean that even if a man's sins were so numerous that they reached to God's very Throne, or even if the sin included blasphemy or the denial of God Himself, repentance can still bring about reconciliation. 'There is nothing that stands in the way of repentance,' i.e. there is no sin which bars the way of sincere repentance, is a commonly held Rabbinic view. The Rabbis debated whether the repentant sinner or the man who had never sinned is the greater. Some Rabbis teach that the repentant sinner is the greater for he had to fight his way through to goodness. The Rabbis believed that a man can 'acquire eternal life in an hour,' i.e. that an hour of reflection leading to sincere repentance can alter completely the whole course of a man's life. Repentance out of fear, teach the Rabbis, has the effect of turning a man's wilful sins into unwitting sins but repentance out of love transforms a man's sins (even his wilful ones) so that they are accounted as merits!

The Rabbis, as we have noted above, gave great prominence to the teaching that neither *Yom Kippur* nor repentance can atone for offences against one's neighbour until the injured person has been appeased. Arising out of this teaching it is the practice of Jews to ask forgiveness of each other on the eve of *Kippur*. Although the victim should be ready to forgive it was said that this did not apply where a man had been the victim of malicious slander. However, it is told of R. Zalman of Volhozhyn, a disciple of the great Gaon of Vilna, that he once overheard a man begging his neighbour for pardon on the eve of *Yom Kippur* only to have his advances rejected. R. Zalman asked the man who refused to forgive why he was so hard-hearted. 'But this man has maliciously slandered me,' was the reply 'and I have no obligation to forgive him.' 'True,' retorted R. Zalman, 'you have no obligation to forgive him. But in a few hours' time you will beg God for His forgiveness. Has He an *obligation* to forgive you? Is it not that you will cast yourself on His mercy as we all do? How can you expect God not to insist on strict justice if you yourself insist on it?.'

Repentance, prayer and charity, these, says the well-known *Yom Kippur* hymn, 'avert the evil decree.' It is by the practice of these that man is led back to God. Through repentance, say the Jewish teachers, man becomes a 'new creature.' His life is renewed. Its quality is changed. He is no longer the same person. 'Repent one day before your death,' said a Rabbi to his pupils. When they asked him how can a man know the day of his death he explained that this was precisely his meaning: that a man should spend all his days in repentance. In the course of their praises during the Tabernacle's celebrations it is recorded in the Talmud that the men whose whole lives had been spent in good living would say: 'Happy our youth that has not disgraced our old age.' The penitents among them would say, however, 'Happy our old age which has atoned for our youth.' Both would say: 'Happy is he who hath not sinned, but let him who hath sinned return and He will pardon him.'

The spirit of authentic Jewish teaching is found in the following Midrash. 'They asked Wisdom: "What is the sinner's punishment?" Wisdom replied: "The soul that sinneth, it shall die." (*Ez.* xviii: 20). They asked the Torah: "What is the sinner's punishment?" The Torah replied: "He shall bring a guilt offering and it shall atone for him." (*Lev.* i: 4). Then they asked God Himself: "What is the sinner's punishment?" And God replied: "Let him repent and all will be forgiven." As it is said: "Good and upright is the Lord; Therefore doth He instruct sinners in the way." (*Ps.* xxv: 8). "My children," God says, "what do I require of you? Seek Me and live!" '